KONGO

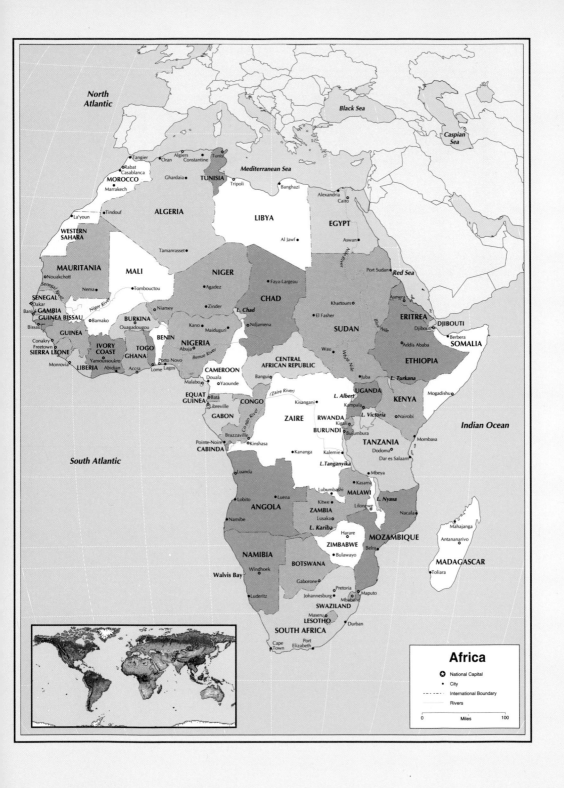

North
Atlantic

Black Sea

Caspian
Sea

Mediterranean Sea

Tangier
Algiers
Oran
Constantine
Tunis
Rabat
Casablanca
TUNISIA
MOROCCO
Ghardaia
Tripoli
Banghazi
Marrakech
Alexandria
Cairo

La'youn
Tindouf
ALGERIA
LIBYA
EGYPT

WESTERN
SAHARA
Tamanrasset
Al Jawf
Aswan

MAURITANIA
MALI
NIGER
Faya-Largeau
Port Sudan
Red Sea

Nouakchott
Agadez
Asmera

Nema
Tombouctou
Zinder
CHAD
Khartoum
ERITREA
DJIBOUTI

SENEGAL
Dakar
Niamey
L. Chad
El Fasher
Djibouti
Berbera

GAMBIA
Bamako
Kano
Maiduguri
Ndjamena
Wau
Addis Ababa
SOMALIA

GUINEA BISSAU
BURKINA
Ouagadougou
NIGERIA
SUDAN
ETHIOPIA

Bissau
GUINEA
BENIN
Abuja
Benue River
CENTRAL
L. Turkana

Conakry
Freetown
IVORY
COAST
TOGO
GHANA
Porto Novo
CAMEROON
AFRICAN REPUBLIC
Juba

SIERRA LEONE
Yamoussoukro
Lome
Lagos
Douala
Bangui
UGANDA
Mogadishu
KENYA

Monrovia
LIBERIA
Abidjan
Accra
Yaounde
L. Albert
Kampala

EQUAT
GUINEA
Malabo
Bata
(Zaire River)
L. Victoria
Nairobi

GABON
Libreville
CONGO
Kisangani
RWANDA
Kigali
Mombasa

Pointe-Noire
Brazzaville
ZAIRE
BURUNDI
Bujumbura
TANZANIA
Indian Ocean

CABINDA
Kinshasa
Kananga
Kalemie
Dodoma
Dar es Salaam

South Atlantic
Luanda
L.Tanganyika
Mbeya

Lubumbashi
Kasama
MALAWI
L. Nyasa

Lobito
Luena
Kitwe
Lilongwe
Nacala

Namibe
ANGOLA
ZAMBIA
Lusaka
MOZAMBIQUE

L. Kariba
Harare
Mahajanga

NAMIBIA
ZIMBABWE
Bulawayo
Beira
Antananarivo

Windhoek
BOTSWANA
MADAGASCAR

Walvis Bay
Gaborone
Pretoria
Maputo
Toliara

Luderitz
Johannesburg
Mbabane
SWAZILAND

Maseru
LESOTHO
Durban

SOUTH AFRICA

Cape
Town
Port
Elizabeth

Africa

⊛ National Capital

• City

--- International Boundary

—— Rivers

0   Miles   100

The Heritage Library of African Peoples

KONGO

Chika Okeke, M.F.A.

THE ROSEN PUBLISHING GROUP, INC.
NEW YORK

Published in 1997 by The Rosen Publishing Group, Inc.
29 East 21st Street, New York, NY 10010

Copyright 1997 by The Rosen Publishing Group, Inc.

First Edition

Manufactured in the United States of America

Library of Congress Cataloging-in-Publication Data

Okeke, Chika.
    Kongo / Chika Okeke. — 1st ed.
        p.   cm. — (The heritage library of African peoples)
    Includes bibliographical references and index.
    Summary: A look at the culture, history, and contemporary life of the Kongo people of the Republic of Congo, western Zaire, and northern Angola.
    ISBN 0-8239-2001-1
    1. Kongo (African people)—Juvenile literature.   [1. Kongo (African people) 2. Africa—Social life and customs.]   I. Title. II. Series.
    DT650.K66034   1996
    967—dc20   96-7892
                                                                   CIP
                                                                    AC

Contents

INTRODUCTION

THERE IS EVERY REASON FOR US TO KNOW something about Africa and to understand its past and the way of life of its peoples. Africa is a rich continent that has for centuries provided the world with art, culture, labor, wealth, and natural resources. It has vast mineral deposits, fossil fuels, and commercial crops.

But perhaps most important is the fact that fossil evidence indicates that human beings originated in Africa. The earliest traces of human beings and their tools are almost two million years old. Their descendants have migrated throughout the world. To be human is to be of African descent.

The experiences of the peoples who stayed in Africa are as rich and as diverse as of those who established themselves elsewhere. This series of books describes their environment, their modes of subsistence, their relationships, and their customs and beliefs. The books present the variety of languages, histories, cultures, and religions that are to be found on the African continent. They demonstrate the historical linkages between African peoples and the way contemporary Africa has been affected by European colonial rule.

Africa is large, complex, and diverse. It encompasses an area of more than 11,700,000 square miles. The United States, Europe, and India could fit easily into it. The sheer size is an indication of the continent's great variety in geography, terrain, climate, flora, fauna, peoples, languages, and cultures.

Much of contemporary Africa has been shaped by European colonial rule, industrialization, urbanization, and the demands of a world economic system. For more than seventy years, large regions of Africa were ruled by Great Britain, France, Belgium, Portugal, and Spain. African peoples from various ethnic, linguistic, and cultural backgrounds were brought together to form colonial states.

For decades Africans struggled to gain their independence. It was not until after World War II that the colonial territories became independent African states. Today, almost all of Africa is ruled by Africans. Large numbers of Africans live in modern cities. Rural Africa is also being transformed, and yet its people still engage in many of their customs and beliefs.

Contemporary circumstances and natural events have not always been kind to ordinary Africans. Today, however, new popular social movements and technological innovations pose great promise for future development.

George C. Bond, Ph.D., Director
Institute of African Studies
Columbia University, New York

Today, many Kongo are members of alternative religious groups that combine Christian beliefs with traditional religion. Seen here are prophets of the Church of the Holy Spirit in Africa.

1

THE LAND AND THE PEOPLE

BAKONGO, WHICH MEANS THE KONGO
people, live mainly in the modern countries of
Angola, Congo, and Zaire. Their total population is about 5 million.

In fact Bakongo consist of several closely
related peoples who share a similar culture. But
differences between them can be noticed, for
example, in the different dialects of the Kikongo
language that they speak. The Kongo peoples
also have strong historical ties to the powerful
Kongo Kingdom. This wealthy kingdom
flourished from about 1390 until its defeat by
the Portuguese in 1678.

The Portuguese first made contact with the
Kongo Kingdom in 1483. From that date on
these two countries were closely linked by trade,
and also by religion. The Kongo king and many
of his nobles were baptized as Christians in

1491. Christianity became the official state religion in the 1500s, and was promoted throughout the kingdom. Portuguese missionaries worked at turning Bakongo away from their own religion and converting them to Christianity. Kongo princes and nobles were sent to the courts of the king of Portugal and of the Pope in Rome. The Kongo Kingdom became famous throughout Europe.

The wealth of the Kongo Kingdom was based on the labor of its slaves and its control over local resources, neighboring peoples, and trade. At the peak of its power, it dominated a vast area on both sides of the mighty Congo (or Zaire) River, and from the Atlantic coast to the Kwango River far inland. Goods were brought to the capital, Mbanza Kongo, by boats on the Congo River and its branches. Other trade and transport routes were carved through the dense tropical rain forests and savannas that are found in the region.

Some important goods that flowed to the capital were iron, copper, cloth made from bark, salt, and products from cattle and wild animals. But the key to the kingdom's wealth was labor. Slaves farmed the fields around the capital, worked on public projects for the king, such as buildings, served the king and his nobles, and made up the army. Although these Bakongo slaves had to work for the nobility, they were

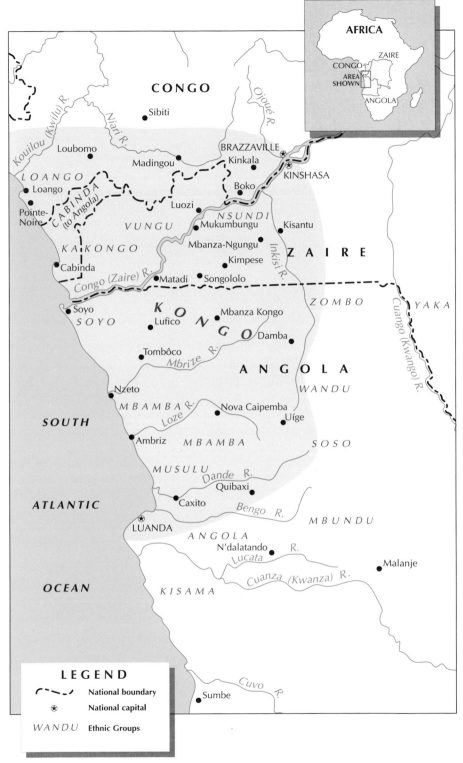

The Kongo peoples are found in the countries of Congo, Zaire, and Angola.
The Congo (or Zaire) River is the main feature of the region.

European missionaries have attempted to convert Kongo peoples to Christianity from the late 1400s until today. Some Kongo have embraced Christianity, while others have retained their traditional beliefs. Still others, like these pilgrims at Simon Kimbangu's mausoleum at Nkamba-Jerusalem, have turned to alternative religions that combine Christian and traditional beliefs.

allowed to set up their own households. Their lives were not that different from Bakongo people who farmed in areas far from the capital.

Contact with Europeans had a great impact on the Kongo Kingdom, and eventually destroyed it. The relationship with the Portuguese became competitive and hostile during the 1500s and 1600s. The Portuguese undermined the power and wealth of the kingdom. The population of the region was greatly reduced because the Portuguese seized millions of slaves, many of them Bakongo subjects. Further, thousands of Bakongo died from epidemics of new diseases introduced by the Portuguese.

Slaves from the Bakongo region were taken by the Portuguese to work on plantations in Brazil and other parts of the Americas. The slaves preserved many aspects of Kongo culture in the Americas, and these Bakongo roots still play a strong role in the Americas today.

The violence and destruction caused by slavery in the Kongo region lasted into the 1880s. By then the Kongo region was firmly under European control. During the century of European colonization, which lasted until the 1960s, Africans had almost no freedoms and they suffered greatly. Labor conditions were so bad that workers were treated much like slaves.

Today most rural Kongo people are farmers, growing tropical crops such as yams, cassava (a root vegetable like sweet potatoes), plantains, and oil palms. Hunting, fishing, keeping live-stock, and trading surplus items at markets are also important. Now many Bakongo work in the cities and towns of the modern countries of Angola, Congo, and Zaire, and in other parts of the world. Many African Americans also share a Bakongo heritage, although these Kongo roots might be hard to pinpoint now.▲

2

HISTORY

THE KONGO KINGDOM WAS FOUNDED ABOUT
1390 by Nimi a Lukeni. He conquered the
region around Mbanza Kongo and made his
capital there.

At this time there were several other small
states in the region. They included Soyo, at the
mouth of the Congo River, which became the
main Kongo port, and the Mbata state on the
eastern side of the Inkisi River. These two states
soon became the closest allies of the Kongo, and
their rulers intermarried with the Kongo royal
family.

The Kongo Kingdom expanded by defeating
neighboring groups or creating alliances with
them, especially through marriage. By the late
1400s, the Kongo king headed a complex state
with several provinces. Many provinces were
ruled directly by relatives of the king or by
nobles who were favored by the king. Others
continued to have their own rulers, but they

accepted the authority of the Kongo king. Often they hoped to bind themselves more closely to the king, known as the Mani Kongo, by marrying into his family line.

▼ THE COMING OF THE PORTUGUESE ▼

In 1483, the Portuguese navigator Diogo Cão became the first European explorer to make direct contact with the Kongo king. Five years later, the king of Portugal sent royal ambassadors to the Kongo court at Mbanza Kongo. A friendly relationship developed between the Mani Kongo, Nzinga a Nkuwu, and the Portuguese king, John II.

Nzinga allowed some of his royal princes, who were taught to speak Portuguese, to convert to Christianity. This gesture of openness strengthened ties between the two countries. After this meeting, Portuguese traders began to arrive in the Kongo Kingdom to buy ivory, wax, copper, and palm oil. In return for these goods, they offered mirrors, beads, snuff boxes, guns, and gun-powder to the Kongo.

▼ CHRISTIANITY IN THE KINGDOM ▼

The Mani Kongo did not at first fully embrace Christianity. The Kongo ruler Nzinga allowed some of his princes to travel to Portugal, but Nzinga himself only half-heartedly converted to Christianity in 1491.

The Kongo were in contact with Europeans from the late 1400s.
Seen here is a drawing of the Loango capital on the Atlantic coast,

published in the 1600s. Loango, founded in the 1100s, served as
the main port for the early Atlantic trade with central Africa.

A Portuguese delegation was sent to Mbanza Kongo to baptize Nzinga a Nkuwu in 1491. They were received by a crowd of thousands, led by the members of the court. The king sat on a throne of carved ivory and wood, which was placed on a high platform. He wore a beautifully decorated, tall crown, or *mpu*, made from finely woven palm fiber. His other royal regalia, or symbols, included a brass bracelet, and the tail of a wild animal.

After his baptism Nzinga took the Portuguese name Joao I. Just before he died in 1506, Nzinga and his favorite son, Mpanzu a Kitima, decided to abandon Christianity. The queen and another prominent prince, Nzinga a Mbemba, remained Christian. The Kongo royal house was thus divided, and the two princes went to war with each other.

Mpanzu's army was larger than his rival's, but according to legend, Mbemba's army was led by an angel and a heavenly knight with a red cross. When Mpanzu's army saw the knight and the angel, they fled in fear. The following day, Mpanzu attacked again, but the knight and angel intervened again. That same day, Mpanzu stepped on some poisoned stakes, which had been set into the ground by his enemy, and died. Following the death of their leader, Mpanzu's men fled the city, and Nzinga a Mbemba became king.

King Afonso I played an important role in bringing the Christian religion to the Kongo region, a tradition which continues today. Seen here is a missionary at work in modern-day Zaire.

The new king changed his name to Afonso I. He ordered all of his chiefs and nobles to become Christians. He chose a European name for the capital city: São Salvador. He also ordered the burning of all religious objects used in Kongo ceremonies, such as masks and statues. All those who refused to convert were punished. So many churches were built in São Salvador that the city was nicknamed Ekogo dia Ngungo, which means the city of church bells.

In addition to churches Afonso I ordered the building of schools. The Kongo king learned to read and write Portuguese himself and continued to send his sons to Portugal for schooling. His son Dom Henrique became the Bishop of Utica in what is now Tunisia. Dom Henrique returned to his homeland in 1521 and became the Bishop of Kongo.

Because the king converted to Christianity and allowed Portuguese traders and missionaries to enter his territory freely, he enjoyed a close relationship with King Manuel of Portugal, who ruled from 1495 to 1521. King Manuel referred to Afonso as his royal "brother." The two wrote to each other regularly and exchanged gifts to show their mutual friendship and respect.

This friendship and peace, however, did not last. The Portuguese merchants brought books, printers, and other beneficial imports to Africa. But they schemed to take control of the region's trade routes away from the Mani Kongo. Also their greed for slaves soon caused turmoil.

▼ THE SLAVE TRADE ▼

The Kongo Kingdom played an important role in the slave trade for several reasons. The Portuguese needed slaves to work on their large plantations in Brazil. Most of these slaves came from the west coast of Africa. Since the Mani Kongo was very powerful, the Portuguese needed his permission to transport slaves from the interior of the continent. In return, the Mani Kongo profited from his control of the slave trade. As long as he cooperated with the Portuguese, the Kongo king would stay in power. The Kongo themselves also enslaved other Africans from neighboring states. One Kongo king, called Alvaro II (1587–1614), was reported to have between 15,000 and 20,000 Tio slaves in his personal guard force.

The Portuguese also kidnapped and forced many Kongo people into slavery. They tried to hide this from Afonso I. Afonso became alarmed by the many complaints that reached his ears about the slave traders' brutal behavior in his kingdom and against his own people. The situation became worse when several Kongo princes, sent to Portugal for religious training, were kidnapped by pirates. They never returned.

In 1521, John III became king of Portugal. Afonso I wrote to ask John III to stop the slave traders from kidnapping his people. But Afonso's letter was never answered, and the friendship between the two kingdoms began to sour. More slave traders entered the Kongo Kingdom, often forcing the healthiest Kongo men and women onto slave ships that carried them far from home, never to return. By the 1880s, when slavery came to an official end in the region, perhaps as many as 5 million men, women, and children had been seized and many of them died.

By the time King Afonso I died in 1561, the kingdom was in serious trouble. As Afonso lost control over the trade routes, other Kongo chiefs began to take part in the profitable slave trade. This further undermined the Mani Kongo's authority.

▼ TROUBLE IN THE KINGDOM ▼

The slave trade was not the only crisis in the kingdom. Another problem arose from the Portuguese trade in *nzimbu*, a kind of seashell. In the markets, people bought goods with these shells, which were the currency of the old Kongo Kingdom. Previously, the Mani Kongo had controlled the amount of *nzimbu* currency on the market. Portuguese traders brought vast quantities of these shells into the country, causing inflation. This made the *nzimbu* practically worthless. The Mani Kongo lost control of the economy of the kingdom.

Another major problem was that of succession. After King Afonso I's death, several princes competed for the throne. In the past, very few princes were eligible to replace the Mani Kongo. This was because royal princes were only allowed to marry their royal cousins. According to the teachings of the Catholic Church, such marriages were sinful. After converting, the princes had to marry more distant relatives. The palace was soon filled with members of different Kongo families that were potential competitors for the throne. Until the kingdom collapsed 200 years later, royal princes fought each other for control. This power struggle weakened the kingdom.

▼ WAR WITH THE PORTUGUESE ▼

Despite friction between their two countries,

the Portuguese and the Kongo maintained an uneasy peace. In 1575 the Portuguese moved most of their trading operations south to Luanda. This gave the Mani Kongo even less control over the important trade routes. In the same year, the Portuguese seized control of a huge territory called Angola, which included land from the southern part of the Kongo Kingdom.

It did not take long for other European powers to come to the Kongo region in search of slaves, ivory, and copper. The Dutch came in 1641 and seized Luanda from the Portuguese. Since the Dutch never gained control of the interior trade routes, however, they were unable to make use of their new territory and withdrew seven years later.

By 1650, the relationship between the Mani Kongo and the Portuguese was in danger of a complete collapse. A dispute broke out between the Mani Kongo and some of his subjects who were living near Luanda and wanted control over some local copper mines. When the Portuguese sided with these rebels, Mani Kongo Antonio gathered his army and went to war. With their more powerful army, the Portuguese easily defeated the Kongo Kingdom. The Kongo Kingdom quickly fell apart as chiefs and princes competed for power. The capital was adandoned in 1678.

In 1704 a Kongo prophetess called Dona Beatriz failed in an attempt to restore the

Both the Portuguese and the Dutch traded with the Kongo Kingdom. This illustration shows a Dutch delegation visiting the Kongo king Garcia II in 1642, shortly after the Dutch seized Luanda from the Portuguese. The king's secretary writes at his knee. Behind the king is a fancy hanging given to the previous king by the Portuguese.

kingdom. Even though the kingdom was destroyed, the Kongo people continued to recognize their line of kings until the last king died in the 1930s. Many Bakongo continued to take pride in the Kongo Kingdom, though its power had passed, and hoped to revive it. Even today, some Kongo still believe the kingdom will rise again.▲

chapter

3

KONGO SOCIETY

BY CHOICE, OR BECAUSE OF HISTORIC AND
modern changes, many Kongo no longer live in
rural villages or follow their old customs. Many
live in cities, wear Western clothes, and no
longer follow their traditional religion. The
modern countries of Zaire and Angola have
encouraged their people to move away from traditional values. However, these values and customs still influence society in many ways.

In traditional Kongo society, each individual
has a unique role to play within the family
kanda, or lineage. Men and women have specific
responsibilities in Kongo culture, which children
learn as they grow up.

▼ LINEAGE POLITICS ▼

In Kongo society, the *kanda* traces its descent
through the female line. This means that children are closer to their uncles on their mother's
side than to their own fathers. Each *kanda* is

Today, few Kongo live in traditional villages, like the one pictured here. Regardless of where they live, most Kongo people still uphold the traditions of their *kanda*, or lineage.

ruled by a headman who imposes rules and keeps peace among his people. When disputes arise, members of the *kanda* are invited to settle the problem. For serious problems, diviners may be called upon to help.

Each family line has its own *minsiku* (singular: *nsiku*), or set of rules, to guide them. Many *minsiku* have been handed down from generation to generation, and are as old as a family's ancestors. The *minsiku* regulate lineage activities such as how to divide farmland and whether to use wood for timber or for firewood. Each age group has its own *minsiku*.

The headman is responsible for enforcing these *minsiku*. Anyone who disobeys is punished.

▼ EARLY CHILDHOOD ▼

From the time of its birth until its fifth or sixth birthday, a child remains in the care of its mother. There was a high rate of infant and child mortality in the past, so childhood was often a time of worry for children's parents. Kongo mothers, like those in other cultures, did everything possible to keep their babies in good health. Children were taken to the *nganga* (diviner), who had knowledge of both medical and spiritual matters.

It is the duty of every mother to teach her child the important things about the family and the *kanda*. She tells stories, sometimes in the form of songs, concerning family history. These stories teach the child the differences between good and bad behavior. They also help the child learn Kikongo. It is through the mother that the child begins to understand his or her place in the world.

▼ GIRLS AND BOYS ▼

When a child reaches the age of six, the mother ceases to be the center of its life. At that age, a boy begins to sleep in the men's lodge and a girl goes to the women's lodge. In traditional Kongo society, men and women, even married couples, do not live together in the same houses. Children learn quickly about the different roles played by each gender in Kongo

KINSHIP IN THE KONGO KINGDOM

Traditional Kongo society is matrilineal, meaning that descent and inheritance are traced through the female line. At puberty, male children go to live with their maternal uncle, while females prepare for marriage at home. When the uncle dies, his property passes to his nieces and nephews. The matrilineal system also protects mothers and children.

If a father neglects or abuses his family, his wife reminds him that he is an outsider and that her main loyalty is to her *kanda*. If the man does not improve, the family can turn to the children's maternal uncles for help.

This does not mean that the father has no rights of his own. Aside from receiving part of the bride-price, the father and his *kanda* play an important role in the life of his children. Occasionally when a man rises to a position of importance, his children want to have a closer relationship with him than with their maternal uncles. Further, the father's family is credited with having great spiritual powers over the children. If a child is ill, the father's family might be consulted to break a curse or provide a cure.

culture. Other people, including the child's peers, begin to play important roles in the child's life.

A boy soon discovers all the privileges that belong to a male child. He shifts his attention away from his mother. Now in the constant company of his father, a boy learns the rules and tricks needed for hunting and other male tasks. A father teaches his son how to act like a

In Kongo society, boys begin to learn their distinct roles in society at an early age. These young boys walk between two parts of Kisiasia village in Manianga.

Kongo men and women each have specific tasks to perform in the *kanda*. Seen here are Kongo women preparing a meal at an outdoor kitchen (top) and others preparing a field for farming (bottom).

man both in his family and within the *kanda*.
Often a boy serves as an apprentice in his
father's profession. He also studies other topics,
such as traditional Kongo religious ceremonies
and customs.

As a boy reaches puberty, however, he leaves
his father's house to live with his mother's
brother, who is responsible for the child from
then on. In matrilineal societies, the family line
is traced through female ancestors, so the
mother's relatives are of great importance. A
young man is the heir of his maternal uncle,
with whom he is very close. While the father still
plays a role in providing bride-price and other
activities, he is largely removed from the responsibilities of child-rearing.

A young girl continues living with and learn-
ing from her mother until she marries and leaves
for her husband's house. She learns how to keep
a home, how to cook the tastiest dishes, how to
grow food on the farm, and how to be a good
wife and mother. The sooner she learns these
skills, the sooner she will attract suitors. Since
an unmarried girl receives little respect, and a
young mother is the pride of the *kanda*, early
marriages are an advantage in the traditional
Kongo view.

▼ PREPARATION FOR MARRIAGE ▼
In the past, a young Kongo girl had special

training to prepare for marriage. This was mainly given during the girls' initiation school, which took place during puberty. All the girls who had come of age were taken to a special house called *nzo kumbi*. Nobody was allowed to see the girls during this period except their female teachers. This period lasted for one year or more.

In the *nzo kumbi* the girls were treated with great care and fed fine food. Their young bodies were conditioned to bring out their beauty. A red dye was made by mixing a local powder called *tukula* with palm oil. The initiates then covered their bodies with the dye. They also wore decorations such as copper or brass bangles, necklaces, and waist bands made of glass beads.

The young women learned dances and songs. At the end of their stay in the *nzo kumbi*, they performed these songs for the entire *kanda*. During this graduation celebration, a young woman was often approached by suitors bearing gifts. These gifts were given to the girl's mother, who received them for her daughter. The mother chose the best suitors to court the newly initiated young woman.

Just before the marriage ceremony, the girls went back to the *nzo kumbi* for a final ceremony. They then led a procession to the river, where the young women bathed. This bath removed the *tukula* from their bodies and showed their readiness for marriage.

During Kongo marriages, the bride observes many customs and traditions. To show her reluctance of leaving her parents' home, the bride had hidden herself from the groom's family. However, when she was found, she was dressed in her finest clothes and had her suitcase packed. Seen above the bride (center) and the women from the groom's family form a ceremonial parade to welcome her into her new village.

▼ THE MARRIAGE CEREMONY ▼

Today traditional Kongo marriages are arranged by the families of the betrothed. Both the father's *kanda* and the mother's *kanda* must agree to the marriage. The bride is blessed by all of her relatives, but the most important blessing comes from her father's mother's *kanda*. This blessing protects the bride from curses and other evils. Without these blessings, the young wife might not be able to have children.

After the blessings, the bridegroom pays the bride-price to his wife's family. This payment recognizes the family's loss of a family member and their role in raising her. The final steps in the Kongo marriage include a feast and dancing. ▲

chapter

4

RELIGION AND MEDICINE

IT IS HARD TO GENERALIZE ABOUT KONGO
beliefs because they have changed a great deal
over the centuries. Today, people's beliefs vary
widely and may differ from the traditions discussed here.

Spirits are very important in traditional
Kongo belief: invisible spirits who live in this
world and other spirits that live outside of it.
Both types of spirits play vital roles in the life of
an individual or of entire communities.

The world is divided into three parts for
human beings, their ancestors, and the spirits.
Land is the first part, where human beings live
with all of the evil forces. The land is associated
with charcoal, or *kala*, representing chaos and
evil. The second part is known as Mpemba,
or the land of the dead, where ancestors live
with other natural forces. The Kongo rely on

Different colors of earth are important symbols in Kongo religion. In this photograph, pilgrims view portions of white river clay and red earth. These have been prepared for them to take home for healing uses.

ancestral spirits to protect them from evil and help them during crises. Mpemba is associated with white river clay, or *luvemba*, and water, a symbol of clarity and light. It is also the part that fights the evil forces in the world. The third part is the sky, where other spiritual forces exist.

There are two different beliefs about the most important deities. The first is that there is one all-powerful Supreme Being, Nzambi Mpungu. He is the creator of the world and all power in the world comes from Him. (It should be noted that Nzambi Mpungu only came to be regarded as male after Christianity was introduced.) Since nobody has ever seen Nzambi Mpungu, there are no images of Him in the Kongo region. Nzambi Mpungu is never worshipped nor given sacrifices, since prayers cannot reach Him. Contact with Him must be made through lesser spirits and the ancestors, who control the destinies of human beings.

The less popular second belief is that there are two major deities, one male and one female. In this view, Nzambi Mpungu remains supreme but is joined by Nzambi, his daughter. According to this view, Nzambi Mpungu was the sky god, while Nzambi was the earth goddess. Nzambi Mpungu created the world but remained in the sky; he sent his daughter to look after the earth. It did not take long, however, for Nzambi Mpungu to come down to the earth. When he saw how much his daughter enjoyed it, he decided to marry her and live there. Their children became the human race.

The belief in Nzambi Mpungu as the single, male Supreme Being is more widely accepted today. This may be a result of the influence of Christian missionaries who also believed in one male Supreme Being. In many Kongo Christian

NZAMBI AND THE CRAB

There are many stories that tell of how Nzambi made the various animals look and behave as they do. One story describes the creation of the Crab, who is considered a mediator between the living and the dead. This is because he lives both above and below the sand.

One day long, long ago, Nzambi, the earth goddess, was invited to a town to settle a dispute. While she was in the town listening to both sides of the argument, she heard the sound of a drum. The drumbeat was a sign that someone else had a dispute that required mediation. She listened again and recognized the sound of her own *ndunguzilo*, or great drum. She immediately sent Pig to run back to her town and find out who was beating her drum. Pig went and soon returned to tell Nzambi that he found no one beating the drum.

When the drum sounded again, Nzambi sent Antelope to find out who was beating it. Antelope galloped away and later returned with another disappointing report. He claimed that no one was beating the drum.

Nzambi was very distressed. She ordered everyone to go with her to find out who was beating the drum. When they got to where the drum was, everyone hid in the bushes nearby. After a short time, Crab crawled out of his hole, climbed the drum, and beat it with his claws. Immediately, Nzambi and the others jumped out of the bushes and caught him.

Anger filled the voice of Nzambi as she scolded the mischievous Crab. She told Crab that he had behaved like someone who had no head. As his punishment, she said that Crab and all his descendants would be headless. His second punishment was that human beings would find his meat sweet and would always hunt him for food.

churches God is called Nzambi, meaning the
male Nzambi Mpungu.

▼ *MINKISI* ▼

The Kongo appeal to many
spirits and lesser gods to
help solve their problems.
Shrines, medicines, and
sacred objects are
dedicated to these
invisible deities. Sacred
objects are the visible
representatives of the
spirits behind them.
These objects are
known as *minkisi*
(singular: *nkisi*)
and are commonly
used in the tradi-
tional religion of
the Kongo and
some other African
groups.

The first *nkisi*
came from Nzambi

Minkisi (singular: *nkisi*) are sacred religious sculptures that play a
key role in dealing with the spirit world. Seen here is an *nkisi*
statuette adorned with feathers, glass, metal, animal teeth, shells,
and cloth.

but, according to Kongo religious history, it was Funza, the god of twins, who created it. Even today it is believed that the best *minkisi* are made by the parents of twins.

Minkisi can take various forms, including statuettes, pouches, or bags filled with special herbs and medicines. If an *nkisi* does not have medicinal items attached, it has no power.

Minkisi are not worshipped directly. Instead, they are concentrated on when someone prays. Each is made for a particular purpose and has a specific form. Any *nkisi* must take the traditional form of *minkisi* used for that same purpose in the past. Specific objects and herbs must be brought together in a particular way before an *nkisi* is created. Special ceremonies and songs must be performed. If they are not done properly, the spirit to whom the *nkisi* is dedicated could become angry. The *nkisi* might turn out to be weak or useless. An angry spirit may even make an *nkisi* do the wrong things. Since the *nkisi* itself serves only to focus a person's prayer to the spirits, an *nkisi* can be thrown away when it no longer seems to work.

▼ DISEASE AND THE POWER ▼ OF THE WORD

Most Kongo believe that words have great power; even casual wishes can be taken seriously by the spirits. Some gossip is seen as a type of intentional evil, because negative things said about someone could cause the illness or death of the person discussed. Sometimes Nzambi may make people, especially the elderly, sick. These illnesses are known as "diseases of God." Most diseases, however, are thought to come from the curses and evil wishes of other people. Greed and envy are often responsible.

▼ NKASA AND CRIME DETECTION ▼

In the 1800s Kongo society fell into turmoil as a result of colonial forces. One way the political tension was reflected in society was by an increase in poison ordeals, known as *nkasa*. Poison was given to accused persons to determine their guilt or innocence. Kings in the old Kongo Kingdom are reported to have used *nkasa* to test the loyalty of their governors and lower chiefs. *Nkasa* was also used to ensure that husbands and wives remained faithful.

Nkasa was used as a last resort when other methods, including diviners, failed to identify the guilty person. Suspects were brought to the village square. They were each given equal amounts of a poison prepared from the bark of the *nkasa* tree. As the villagers danced around the suspects, the poison took effect. The first to collapse or faint was declared guilty. Those who survived this ordeal were cleared of all charges.

Diviners are an important part of traditional Kongo society. They are consulted to understand why misfortune affects particular people or groups. The diviner Mama Marie Kukunda, seen here, conducts an interclan reunion to discover the causes of a client's disease.

This and other Kongo customs show the close relationship between medical and spiritual matters that exists in the traditional Kongo view.

▼ DIVINERS ▼

Evil can take various forms, including illness, infertility, and other troubles. People often appeal to spirits to battle evil. At times, however, they also appeal to human specialists who deal with the spirit world. These specialists, or diviners, can see things that ordinary people cannot.

In the past, the most important type of diviner was known as the *nganga ngombo*. This person presided over ceremonies like that involving the *nkasa* poison. When someone was sick, it was the *nganga ngombo* who prescribed the cure.

The term *nganga* (plural: *banganga*) refers to someone who uses herbs and medicines to cure the sick. In Kongo markets today one can still purchase the roots, herbs, animal parts, and other objects used to make medicine. Many medicines are believed to have magical properties.

A *ngunza* (plural: *bangunza*), or prophet, solves problems for both individuals and communities. *Bangunza* communicate with and draw spiritual powers from the ancestors and deities. *Bangunza* use their powers to protect the community from witches and other types of evil.

One person can be both *nganga* and *ngunza*. That person, the *nganga-ngunza*, can discover the both the physical and the spiritual causes of an illness and provide the medicine to cure it.▲

chapter

5

THE ARTS

As in many other societies, the arts play a central role in almost all aspects of Kongo life. Sculpture, music, and dance all contain and transmit cultural values; that is, through the arts people learn about culture. The arts help societies to survive.

▼ SCULPTURE ▼

Kongo artists create many types of sculpture. One common theme is that of the mother and child. Beautifully carved and polished, the sculptures often portray the mother sitting with her legs folded while holding the child on her lap. The carvers emphasize the faces of the women. Some carefully recreate the pointed, filed teeth that were considered a sign of beauty in traditional Kongo society. The sculptures reveal the dignity and beauty of the Kongo mother, and celebrate her fertility.

At left is a *nkisi nkondi*, a hunter figure studded with nails. According to Kongo tradition, driving nails or other sharp objects into a *nkondi* (plural: *minkondi*) stirred the magical power of the figure, causing it to get revenge, track down an evil person, or bring about justice.

The *phemba* figure at right shows Kongo ideas of female beauty, such as the round cheeks, full lips, and delicate chin. Figures like the one pictured here were placed on graves to help the deceased on their way to the afterlife.

Many sculptures are used for religious pur-
poses. These include some *minkisi*, or figures
used to communicate with spirits. *Minkisi*
often have powerful and even fearsome expres-
sions. Some ride on animals while holding
knives or spears. Others have mirrors covering
the sacred medicines that give power to the
sculptures.

Minkondi (singular: *nkondi*), or hunter figures
are a very powerful form of *minkisi*. They are
often studded with nails. *Minkondi* are used to
track down witches, thieves, and other criminals.
Nails are used to irritate the spirit represented
in the *nkondi* until it goes out to find the
wrongdoer.

In the past, when individuals died, they were
buried with certain items. The value of the
burial objects depended on the wealth and status
of the person during life. These things were
believed to be necessities in Mpemba, the land
of the dead. Common burial objects in the past
were *mintadi* figures. Carved from soapstone,
these figures protected the dead from evil
attacks. Legend says that *mintadi* figures could
walk and talk like humans and act as contacts
between the living and the dead.

▼ THE INFLUENCE OF *MINKISI* ▼
ON THE ART OF RENÉE STOUT

Renée Stout is an African American artist

who was born in Kansas in 1958 and raised in Pittsburgh, Pennsylvania, in the United States. While studying art at Carnegie-Mellon University, she began to draw on African sources of inspiration.

Renée Stout paints, sculpts, and makes collages of various objects. Many of her pieces show strong similarities to Kongo art. Some of her sculptures resemble modified *minkisi*. Although they are not made with the same recipe of medicines and ceremonies required in Kongo religion, Stout often adorns her figures with bundles of herbs similar to the medicine bundles that cover some *minkisi*. Others are studded with nails like *minkondi*.

An important aspect of Stout's work that ties it closely to Kongo art is its connection to family and ancestors. Stout has said, "I always had this feeling that the ancestors are there guiding me in some way. . . . I will do things in honor of the ancestor. I let them know that I am accepting their guidance." Many of her other pieces incorporate personal or family objects and momentos, recalling her past and her ancestors', both in the United States and in Africa.

▼ CRAFTS ▼

When Portuguese merchants came to the Kongo region centuries ago, they discovered the quality of Kongo craftsmanship. The woven

CAPOEIRA

Slaves taken to the New World carried their cultures with them. Kongo slaves taken to Brazil contributed to a new, mixed culture. One of their contributions is seen in the Brazilian art of *capoeira*.

Capoeira is variously described as a game, a dance, and a martial art. It includes various ballet-like movements using the feet and the head. Cartwheels, flips, and other acrobatic moves combine with physical blows to form a graceful yet potentially violent contest. By staying low to the ground and balancing on their hands, *capoeristas* (those who practice *capoeira*) can make effective use of their legs and feet. The athleticism and grace of *capoeira* were the root and inspiration of break-dancing, the African American dance style developed in the 1970s and 1980s.

One theory suggests that the slaves who developed *capoeira* often had their hands tied and were forced to discover an alternative method for fighting. In the 1700s and 1800s, *capoeira* earned a reputation in Brazil as a criminal or dangerous sport. It was not until the 1900s, after the formation of several *capoeira* academies and the creation of rules and a code of behavior, that *capoeira* gained respectability.

Many of the terms, names, and moves used in modern *capoeira* are rooted in African traditions. Some of the moves, for example, resemble the way in which Kongo children play.

A *capoeira* contest is performed in a circle known as the *roda*. As the other participants clap and sing, two contestants spar in the center of the circle. Their pace is regulated by the *berimbau* (a bow-like musical instrument that probably originated from from a similar Kongo instrument called a *lungungu*). As the master quickens his pace, so do the contestants.

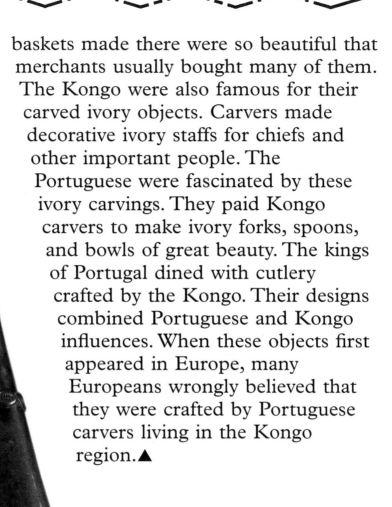

baskets made there were so beautiful that merchants usually bought many of them. The Kongo were also famous for their carved ivory objects. Carvers made decorative ivory staffs for chiefs and other important people. The Portuguese were fascinated by these ivory carvings. They paid Kongo carvers to make ivory forks, spoons, and bowls of great beauty. The kings of Portugal dined with cutlery crafted by the Kongo. Their designs combined Portuguese and Kongo influences. When these objects first appeared in Europe, many Europeans wrongly believed that they were crafted by Portuguese carvers living in the Kongo region.▲

At left is a carved ivory and metal horn, which was played by blowing through the hole in its side. Such horns were used to announce the arrival of royal figures or the coming of a war, or were played at the weddings or funerals of important people.

chapter

6

COLONIALISM AND INDEPENDENCE

THE LOSS OF KONGO DOMINANCE OVER THE slave trade was one of the reasons for the collapse of the Kongo Kingdom in the 1600s. Nevertheless, Kongo trade in slaves and other goods continued for centuries.

By the mid-1800s, slave trading by the British and the Americans had been outlawed. However, many European states continued to exploit the natural resources of Africa. The former Kongo Kingdom had been broken up into many small, independent chiefdoms. The region was tapped for luxury items such as ivory, and raw materials to support Europe's growing industries. In 1884 and 1885 several European governments met in Berlin, Germany to divide Africa among themselves without any input from the Africans.

During the colonial period, great markets developed along trade routes and in large villages. These markets were very similar to the modern-day market above and were an important feature of many African economies.

▼ CONGO FREE STATE ▼

The region inhabited by the Kongo people was divided between Belgium and France, but a large portion of the Kongo region was granted to King Leopold II of Belgium as his personal property. The king named his new property the Congo Free State. Ironically, the people who lived there were anything but free.

King Leopold was a shrewd businessman. He ran his new territory as if it were an industry, producing copper, ivory, and other products. To exploit these resources, Leopold first sought advice from men like the Anglo American explorer Henry Stanley, who had been to the Kongo region. Then he sent his men throughout the region in search of precious natural resources. Every officer who brought in large quantities of materials such as ivory or copper was promoted, but it became a crime for the Kongo to sell these materials to foreigners.

King Leopold's government took what land it wanted, but denied the Kongo the right to own portions of their own land. Belgian officers set up labor camps for the Kongo they had kidnapped from villages. Laborers were forced to work under terrible conditions, building railroads or working on other government projects. In some instances, those who were too sick to work were shot or tied to trees and left to starve. If the officers kept labor costs down, they

Leopold II of Belgium treated the Kongo land under his control as his own property. He forced the Kongo people to work for his benefit and burned villages so that the land could be used for farming. Today, Kongo farmlands are planted with a variety of crops to help fertilize the poor tropical soils.

were rewarded by Leopold's administration.

Belgian troops attacked Kongo villages, seized young men and women to become workers, and looted ivory. Villages were often burned so that the land could be used for farming. Some Kongo women and children were taken hostage to make their relatives work harder. In other cases, hostages were held until their families brought a ransom of rubber or ivory.

Those areas of the Kongo region not suitable for farming did not escape these horrors. There, the Kongo were forced to raise crops to feed the people in the labor camps. If they resisted, they could be punished or killed. By the time Belgium took control of the Congo Free State in 1909, King Leopold had become one of the richest men in the world; but the Kongo and other peoples in the region were devastated. According to some estimates, their population was cut in half. They were poverty-stricken. Never before had the Kongo people seen such misery and death.

▼ BELGIAN COLONIALISM ▼

The Belgian government, recognizing the poor treatment of the Kongo under King Leopold, tried to rebuild the colony. The new Belgian king maintained contact with the Kongo, but appointed a governor-general to manage affairs. Governors, tax collectors, and other officials went to the area to set up a new administration. The governor-general invited local chiefs to take part in the new system, but gave them very little power. While the government claimed it was trying to help the Kongo people, it did little to improve their status. The Belgians, like most Europeans at the time, harbored racist attitudes about African peoples and did not think them fit to govern themselves.

The new administration began to change the lives of the Kongo. The Belgians built churches, schools, and hospitals. Many of the Kongo were moved to mining communities, where they worked for European companies. Unlike King Leopold's camps, workmen received benefits such as basic housing, medical care, and other necessities. In many ways, this new, more lenient regime was as patronizing as King Leopold's, meaning that it treated Africans as inferior. It did not take long for the Kongo to realize that foreign control of their country was unjust.

By the 1920s, more and more Kongo people were openly dissatisfied with the colonial government. In 1926 a Kongo man named Andre Matswa formed a political group, known as the Amicale, to grow the local economies and to benefit the African people.

The Amicale was particularly popular among Kongo living in rural areas. Even though Matswa suffered repeated arrests, his popularity grew. He was so popular that even after his death in 1942 people still voted for him in elections. For more than thirty years, Matswa was a symbol of resistance, used by the Kongo during demonstrations and other acts of protest.

▼ INDEPENDENCE ▼

By 1956, Belgium, along with other European

countries, began to consider turning control of its African colonies over to the local people. The Belgians declared that they would give over control of their colony after thirty more years. After decades of colonial rule, Africans in the region refused to wait.

Some Kongo hoped to establish a new Kongo kingdom. To achieve that goal, they formed the Alliance des Bakongo, or Alliance of the Kongo People (ABAKO), a political party led by Joseph Kasavubu. Many other political parties, based in other regions, soon joined the struggle throughout the colony. One of the most important was the Congo National Movement (MNC), led by Patrice Lumumba.

In January, 1959, a riot occurred in the city of Leopoldville after Belgian officials broke up an ABAKO rally. Colonial officials charged that ABAKO and their supporters who were followers of Simon Kimbangu (the major Kongo prophet of the twentieth century) were to blame. Troops restored order in a brutal fashion, killing dozens and wounding more than 100 people.

By the middle of January, the Belgian government realized it could not keep control for thirty more years. It announced that the colony would become independent soon. A year later, at a conference in Brussels that included many African organizations, they set June 30, 1960, as the date for independence.

Shortly after seizing control of the country's government in 1967, Joseph-Désiré Mobutu changed his name to Mobutu Sese Seko Kuku Ngbendu Wa Za Banga, which means the all-powerful warrior who will go from conquest to conquest, leaving fire in his wake. Zaire's economy has suffered greatly under Mobutu's rule, due in part to the fact that Mobutu has transferred much of the country's wealth into his own personal bank accounts.

Elections were held in 1960. The MNC won a majority. Along with ABAKO, they formed the government, with Kasavubu as president and Lumumba as prime minister. On June 30, 1960, the Democratic Republic of Congo became independent. Today it is known as Zaire.

The years after independence were difficult for the young republic. War broke out in many areas. In 1967, Joseph-Désiré Mobutu seized control of the government and exiled Kasavubu. Since Mobutu is not Bakongo, this political shift effectively marked the end of any hopes for establishing a new Kongo kingdom.

▼ ANGOLA ▼

The Kongo also played a significant role in Angolan politics. In 1954, they formed the Union of Peoples of Northern Angola (UPNA). This was a Kongo-led group dedicated to forming a new Kongo kingdom. In 1957, UPNA petitioned the United Nations for permission to restore the kingdom, an aim shared by ABAKO. By 1962, they realized the impossibility of their dream and became the National Front for the Liberation of Angola (FNLA). They were one of several groups fighting to free Angola from the Portuguese.

When a rival group, the socialist Popular Movement for the Liberation of Angola (MPLA), was elected to govern independent Angola, the antisocialist FNLA set up a government in exile in

Zaire. Led by Holden Roberto, the FNLA fought the elected government. They received support from various sources, including the United States. A rival guerilla group named the Union for the Total Liberation of Angola (UNITA) was born from a split in the FNLA. UNITA later became the main opponent of the popular MPLA government. UNITA was supported mainly by apartheid South Africa. After several years, UNITA and FNLA and their American and South African allies were defeated by the MPLA and their Cuban ally.

During the Angolan Civil War, many Bakongo nationalists fled to Zaire; with the ending of hostilities, most have now returned to Angola.

▼ LIFE IN THE KONGO REGION TODAY ▼

In the past century, dramatic changes have taken place in the Kongo region. The presence of Europeans has deeply affected the traditional way of life. New cities with high-rise buildings have replaced many small towns. Many Kongo have moved from their villages and now work in cities. Villages play a less important role in Kongo life than they once did. Many customs, which do not fit into a modern lifestyle, are no longer practiced.

Some ancient beliefs remain, however. Many city-dwelling and Christian Bakongo still worship their ancestors. Many still say prayers to ancestors during marriage and naming

In modern-day Zaire, some Kongo have retained their traditional lifestyle, living in small villages like Kisiasia (top), home of the Nsundi clan. On the other hand, many Kongo have left these small villages to seek a new life in modern cities, like Matadi (bottom), the main port city on the Congo River.

ceremonies. Some women who have been unable to bear children visit the *banganga* (singular: *nganga*), or diviners, who advertise their services on sign posts in even the biggest cities.

Many Christian churches have combined African and Christian beliefs. In such churches, traditional musical instruments such as drums and rattles, accompany hymn singing. The congregation substitutes Christian names for those of the Kongo spirits in its ceremonies. These churches are another example of how the Kongo have retained much of their cultural identity within a modern world.

Many people continue to respect and offer prayers to their ancestors and regard their problems as coming from evil forces. Major ceremonies are still performed. They may be changed to fit today's circumstances, but the basic beliefs in Nzambi, the ancestors, and the need to overcome evil forces will probably continue into the future. Most Kongo people will always be proud of their ancestors who built one of the most powerful states in central Africa: the great Kingdom of Kongo.▲

Glossary

bride-price Payment to a bride's family made by the groom's family.

colonialism Control of a people or government by a stronger foreign power.

deities Gods or goddesses.

diviner One who communicates with the spirit world.

kanda Clans that have the same female ancestor.

Kikongo Kongo language.

lineage A group tracing its roots from a common ancestor.

Mani Kongo Title for Kongo king.

matrilineal A group tracing its roots through the female line.

minsiku Lineage rules.

ngenda Praise poem.

ngunza Prophet.

nkasa Poison.

nkisi (plural: *minkisi*) Figure that represents spirits and can be used to communicate with them.

nzimbu Shells used as currency in the old Kongo Kingdom.

nzo kumbi Initiation house for girls.

savanna Grassland.

For Further Reading

MacGaffey, Wyatt. "The Eyes of Understanding: Kongo Minkisi." *Astonishment and Power*. Washington, DC: The Smithsonian Institution for the National Museum of African Art, 1993, pp. 21–103.

Challenging Reading

Balandier, Georges. *The Sociology of Black Africa: Social Dynamics in Central Africa*. Translated by Douglas Garman. London: Andre Deutsch, 1970.

Bockie, Simon. *Death and the Invisible Powers: The World of Kongo Belief*. Bloomington: University of Indiana Press, 1993.

Hilton, Anne. *The Kingdom of Kongo*. Oxford: Clarendon Press, 1985.

MacGaffey, Wyatt. *Religion and Society in Central Africa: The Bakongo of Lower Zaire*. Chicago: University of Chicago Press, 1986.

Index

Acknowledgements

The publisher wishes to thank Professor John Janzen. This volume
benefited greatly from both his knowledge of the Kongo people and his
fieldwork photographs of the region.

About the Author

Chika Okeke teaches art history in the Department of Fine Arts at the
University of Nigeria at Nsukka.

RESEARCH John Stoner

PHOTO CREDITS
Cover, pp. 8, 12, 16–17, 24, 26, 29, 30 top, 30 bottom, 33, 35, 40, 50,
52, 59 top, 59 bottom © John Janzen; pp. 19, 56 © Corbis; pp. 38, 44
left, 44 right, 48 © The University of Iowa Museum of Art, The Stanley
Collection.

CONSULTING EDITOR Gary N. van Wyk, Ph.D.

LAYOUT AND DESIGN Kim Sonsky